Things *Come On*

Wesleyan Poetry

Things *Come On*

{ an amneoir }

Joseph Harrington

WESLEYAN UNIVERSITY PRESS

Middletown, Connecticut

Wesleyan University Press

Middletown CT 06459

www.wesleyan.edu/wespress

2011 © Joseph Harrington

All rights reserved

Manufactured in the United States of America

Wesleyan University Press is a member of the Green Press
Initiative. The paper used in this book meets their minimum
requirement for recycled paper.

 This project is supported in part by an award from
the National Endowment for the Arts

Library of Congress Cataloging-in-Publication Data appear
on the last printed page of this book.

5 4 3 2 1

Dedicated to
Elizabeth Peoples Harrington,
and all others
who have fought cancer,
Nixon, or both.

Contents

Acknowledgments

I am very grateful to the College of Liberal Arts and Sciences at the University of Kansas for a sabbatical semester, during which I completed the research for this book and for the others in a series about my mother's life and times. I very much appreciate the interest and care of the editors of the journals in which portions of this work have appeared: David Lazar at *Hotel Amerika*; Andrew Rippeon at *P-Queue*; Chad Lietz & J.D. Mitchell of *Cricket Online Review*; and Charles Jensen at *LOCUSPOINT*.

The author wishes to thank the following parties for their kind permission to quote the following texts:

From *The Cancer Journals* by Audre Lorde. Copyright © 1980, by Audre Lorde; 1997 by Aunt Lute Books. www.auntlute.com

From *Alternatives* by Rose Kushner, by kind permission of Mr. Harvey Kushner.

Illustration, page 14, from Burket, Walter C. (ed.), *Surgical Papers by William Stewart Halsted: 1852–1922* (Plate L), reprinted with kind permission of the Johns Hopkins University Press.

From *Breast Cancer: A Challenging Problem*, ed. M.L. Griem et al. *Recent Results in Cancer Research 42* (New York: Springer-Verlag, 1973). Copyrighted © material from this volume used with kind permission of Springer Science+Business Media.

Thanks also to all those who have read and suggested salubrious changes to this book (or parts of it), especially Susan M. Schultz, Rachel Loden, Judith Roitman, Megan Kaminski, Lyn Hejinian, Ben Lerner, Kevin Rabas, and an anonymous reviewer for Wesleyan University Press. I owe a deep dept of gratitude to Suzanna Tamminen, editor-in-chief at Wesleyan, for her sustained belief in this project, as well as for her editorial guidance.

Most of all, mil gracias a MariaAna Garza, for all her emotional and editorial support over many years. [— "BLJ"]

The sum total of our thoughts creates the world.
  Cecilia Vicuña

The world is everything that happens to me.
  Jean-Michel Espitallier

I prefer to say: I know that I am a human being,
and I know that I have not understood the system.
  Søren Kierkegaard

Things *Come On*

"Your Mother was a Perfect Southern Lady!"

"Bubbly . . . very pleasant person to be around." "Real cheerful, outgoing personality." Very good sense of humor. She got angry, though not frequently. "She was a very feisty woman when she wanted to be." "A redhead." "She wasn't what I'd call pretty, but you didn't notice that, because her personality was so delightful." "She wouldn't stoop to sarcasm. Your mother was the quintessential southern lady." "She was just a very genteel person." "Just a very, very nice lady that anybody would like to be around. But she had a lot of personality and was not the type of person that anyone would walk over at all."

She's always "cheerful" and "out-going." Did she ever express negative emotions to you? I ask. "Oh, no. She was not at all a depressed person. Very upbeat person." Even when she was sick, she didn't complain. *No man wants a sicky wife,* she'd said.

My prosthesis I'd like to offer to the Cancer Soc. as it could sure help someone. Phyllis could do this for you. The size is on the Bra.

— E

I. INVESTIGATION

A TRUE COPY

[A] I watched the Senate hearings in the summer of 1973. My mother lay in the hospital, away, doing nothing. I remember Daniel Inouye and Howard Baker better than I remember her. They left records.

[B] Records indicate she wasn't in the hospital in the summer of 1973, therefore the Senate hearings must have taken place during the summer of 1974.

[C] We watched the Senate hearings together in the summer of 1973, I on the floor in front of the TV, she on the rough avocado-colored upholstery of the couch. She smoked but spoke little. I probably jerked my head around, buck-toothed and cowlicked, to make what I thought were snide and knowing remarks for her approval.

[D] We watched the Senate hearings together, I on the floor in front of the TV, she on the rough avocado-colored upholstery of the couch. I probably jerked my head around, buck-toothed and cow-licked, when she could not resist an arch and knowing remark. She had stopped smoking by then.

[E] No one died, no one resigned. The hearings set this collective, creeping insubstantiality in motion. Senator read it into the *Record* as "hoax" or "ghost."

[F] "Betty Ford's breast cancer, picked up in a routine physical checkup, hit the headlines in early October 1974. The announcement came just months after Nixon's resignation, following the most egregious demonstration of presidential nondisclosure that Americans had ever witnessed."

[G] "SCARE THE SHIT OUT OF THEM!!
SCARE THE SHIT OUT OF THEM!!"

Fall 1972: Birth of Transformed Malignant Daughters.

"I remember how she found out. We had gone to a football game down at Ole Miss. And we were on our way back, and damned highway patrolman gave me a ticket. For speeding. Down somewhere on Highway 7. And, you know, we had passed a speed limit sign, and we were not speeding — I <u>knew</u> that we were not exceeding that speed limit! And after he gave me the ticket, I drove back down and I looked at it. And he'd given me a ticket for going like 45 in a 35 zone, and I drove back down and I looked at it, and it was a 45 mile zone. And the sign said that. And I drove back up there and told him that, and he started calling his supervisor, because he had 'trouble' with somebody out here. So I said, OK fella, forget it. So I was just going to take him down to court. I was going to fight it. And I even called the Highway Department and I was gonna subpoena somebody in the Highway Department to come up there and testify about that sign. I went out and took a picture of the sign. And in the meantime, Lib went to the doctor, and she found out she had this lump in her breast — y'know. I think she knew she had the lump in her breast, and she went to the doctor and found out it was — not good. And I had to go down to court for that thing, and my heart sure wasn't in it by the time I got down there. Well, this moron had found out by the time I got down there. Somebody had clued him in — You friggin idiot, you've given a handful of tickets to people who weren't speeding. So he met me at the door of the courtroom: 'Well, we can cancel that ticket, y'know.' Stupid shit. So anyway, that's how we found out. That was the context."

> (A) "Like all outstanding anniversaries, the precise time a malignant tumor is found has a way of sticking in one's memory."
>
> (B) "It depends on who is telling the story and under what circumstances . . ."

I'll play the subject, if you play the ghost.

This is what they say you say when you first find out:

> *"stomach tightening"*
> stomach *"falling away"*
>
> > *face warm*
>
> *muscles falling away*
>
> > *Drained*
>
> *by a Mack Truck, or*
>
> *a Bolt Out of the Blue.*
>
> > *head seemed to fill with air*
> > *eyes got hot*

Id idn' I didn't feel those things when I found out about <u>her</u>.

    the following steps:

1) "First and foremost among ideational themes reported by patients [and families] is the 'Fear of Death.' If both your sisters died of cancer and the doctor says the word 'cancer' he's saying you're dead you're finished."

2) "I think all three of us were appalled. The scope and size of the project was something that at least in my mind was not envisioned."

3) "Creating a story out of the fragments . . . Repairing the disruption . . . through the function of ordering and categorizing inherent in language."

4) That's why a list is in order.

A memoir is a mirror with a memory. But if memory becomes corrupted and crashes, then order flails to reflect things just as they were:

June 17, 1972 — Watergate burglars arrested.

October 10, 1972 — *Washington Post* reports that FBI has diagnosed pattern of systemic metastatic sabotage conducted by White House biopsy operatives.

November 7, 1972 — Nixon re-elected in landslide. Non-normative nuclear families — cancerous shame face built on sand slide. Mother-made Family, the Beast — the Breast — diseased, covers it up — nuclear family therapy.

SCANDAL

Q: So you would have been ten, when your mother was diagnosed? What did you know, and when did you know it?

" . . . whisked away under cover of darkness and forced to submit to an ordeal cloaked in secrecy . . ."

(mugging squads, kidnapping teams, prostitutes, electronic surveillance, intercepted aircraft communications, espionage, shredding)

"I did know absolutely nothing"

Some New Testament exegetes postulate a missing text, "Q," from which all four gospels were later derived.
Everyone has a Q. Everyone wants it.

Next in your Q, they say you think (to your self):

> *Why is this Me*
> *not Her   you*

> *hapless, not*
> *happening*

> *Not Me.*

> *mirror   warrior   mirage*

> *Why not me? . . .*

> *May-hap   this Not-Me.*

the exegesis:
1) "operation and irradiation are still the subject . . . objective response . . . not predictable . . . not yet been very helpful . . . Obviously, then, the patient presenting with possible mammary cancer cannot wait . . . management of an individual . . . desire to have everything done . . . even at the cost of undesirable complications."

2) Did her doctor explain that cancer meant crab, b/c it was supposed to look like a crab not moving sidewise? I have no oral history on paper from her, so I can neither confirm nor deny.

3) biographical repair of chicken gum chewing wire schmaltzy prosthetic prolepsis . . . Whose repair

4) "We are going to use any means. Is that clear?"

(Surgeons believed in immediate surgery [Today We Know breast cancer does not advance so rapidly], so the mastectomy was probably late 1972, not long after diagnosis. Patients typically signed a "one-step" release form [induced]. The biopsy was conducted while the patient remained anesthetized; if it turned up positive, the surgeon would perform "a radical" then-and-there.)

5) ". . . the famous fingers . . . the rubber gloves with the fingertips."

Today We Know.

Q: But what was she <u>like</u> during this period? Where is Lib in all this? As a Person? How do you remember her?

A: I don't recall. I am sorry. I do not recall. I do not mind telling you any fact that is true.

██████████. One breast was surgically ████████ Her hair fell out quick. In 1972, chemotherapy was a blunt instrument; the ████████

██████ "struggle to speak themselves into existence, without their voices emanating from the great medicojuridical tongue" — the creepy rubber gloves in the margins, holding the documents steady, in other words. Those who speak in silence say a passive voice. Those who spread silences stipulate a 30-year waiting period after their deaths, when the redacted version appears, when the problem seems bigger or smaller, irrelevant. Did they feel "a frustration and a feeling of impotence in being able to deal with the subject"? I know I sure do, suturing text. As an investigator [

From where we stood, we could only hear
the answers, which were amplified.

"The question was, 'Is the author
the narrator, and is the adult
the child of the same name.'"

Please do not answer yes or no.

Q: When did she have the operation?

A: I don't remember . . .

"It's as if the file is missing."

BAPTIST.
Memorial Hospital
Memphis

August 4, 2006

RE: Medical record copies from 1972

Dear Mr. Harrington,

We received a request from you regarding obtaining copies of medical records from 1972. By law we are only required to maintain records for 10 years. We have destroyed all records prior to 1980.

If you have any questions, please contact me at 901-226-2734.

Sincerely,

m, R.H.I.A.

Manager
Health Information Management

"My most vivid recollection, though, is perhaps a little sad. I remember visiting her in the hospital and being totally appalled when she mentioned that her surgeon (whom I knew) left on a . . . trip the day after her surgery. I could never look at him again without feeling angry about that."

believe that the proper thing ever, commence the most signify-
cant impeachment.

his Government since our Founding For the past year allegatio
which has given us the most freedom, President. Some of them
highest standards of living of any come to accept them as facts,
                                    bers of this committee has be
establishment of a precedent which attempt to ascertain wheth

on this country'[...]   he floor of the H
ding Fathers in t   eed be, in the S
ent of three sepa   s of this commit
perform. This sy   s on the other si
work in the futu   **The One-**   k at so
rong Presidents,   **Step:**   am here to tell
eme Courts, all j   "You   ee on Committee
ing the judging.   didn't know   n the members
cular branch, an   whether   and have them
en time, the doc   you'd   eliberations, retr
function and ser   have two or   role as an imp
ouse has seen fit   one,   influences of suc
to remove that o   until you   E, ADA, and simi
removed Andre   woke   o their causes?
only through the   up."   answer is you
ment, or would t   d people of the
ent occupying n   his great Nation

No one can answ[er this question, and this com]mittee detests w
ences of a President's impeachment very nature such things ha
rolled by an opposition party.   be the first in line to punish
Congresses with heavy political United States included, once
initiate or threaten to initiate im-   and I say now, show me the
President of a different political   United States is guilty of the

Illustration. ". . . the code words and the rest of it. I
would have to describe it as

a complete horror story."

Reach to Recovery Lady Eases Patient Suffering With "Pathetic Puff of Lambswool"

Something about *a falsie*. Something about . . . *we're going to get along just fine*. Walking into the house — coming home from the hospital?

Did it occur to me to question "we"? Nowadays, it's always "we're pregnant," with its overtone of male parthenogenesis. But not "we've got breast cancer."

A cosmetic problem. Normal.
Letter to Husbands. Normal.

Upbeat, tight-fitting clothing, which is it, you can't tell!
Look at me — I'm fine. [You?]

Neuralgia → Nostalgia → "prevents a woman . . . from coming to terms with the changed planes of her own body . . . as if it were the result of some crime of which she were guilty."

to question that "fine"? In that season of break-ins, incisions, cover-ups?

"We didn't want Reach to Recovery to become a crutch. . . . We would help the patient for just a few weeks, and then leave her to her own psychological recovery."

The Patient; The Mother; The Woman; The Norn

We didn't want the Wretch to become a witch.
Fine, in fine.   Falsie fine.   The Norm.

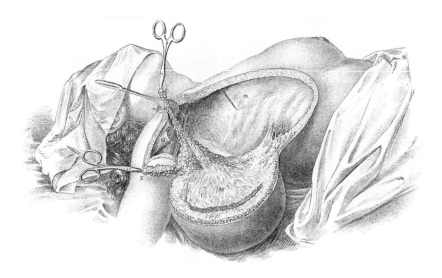

Nixon: It's almost a miracle that I've survived this, you know.
    'Cause I came out of the year '72 terribly tired.
Rosemary Woods: I don't know how you've survived it.
Nixon: And then to have this brutal assault, brutal, brutal, brutal
    assault — day after day after day after day — no let up.

Brutal irony triggers a terrible rage. Nixon for us had always been the
cancer, the cancerer. In America, some one must be to blame. Some
one must die, not always the same one. How create a poem or polity
where the physical is not a trope?

1) Try shaving an armpit you can't feel. You feel the tightness, tin-
    gling, isolation, but something prevents you from speaking.

2) If she really <u>didn't</u> talk to him about it, then she was in fact the
    author of the silence.   And if I didn't ask

3)   [cling to the list like a ladder]

4) "Well, to me, 'clandestine' does not mean illegal, and I can keep a
    secret."

DR. A: "The pain of separation from my breast was at least as sharp as the pain of separating from my mother."

APR 1962

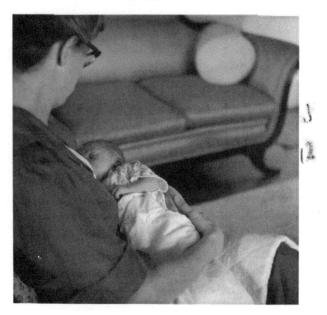

Illustration. "Lib breast feeding Joe — her milk gave him colic, so we had to start feeding him formula from a bottle."

Witness: I can honestly say I recognize the couch, but I have no clue as to what actually happened to it or on it. That is, to the best of my recollection, at this point in time.

DR. B: "Reality-testing . . . proceeds to demand that the loved object no longer exists . . ."   the jury will disregard the picture

DR. C: "[T]he contemporary coagulation of psychoanalytic theory, of religious thinking, and the interested citation from ancient myth and from the classics . . . form a universalizing metanarrative about poetry which reasserts particular conventionalized places for female figures."

ONCE:

She presses back my cuticles with an orangewood stick. It doesn't exactly hurt, but it doesn't exactly feel good.

ONCE:

a long red coat with fox-fur trim I stuck my nose into from the back seat on the way to church; her glove patting my face

ONCE:

She made three wise men from felt — stylized, featureless on burlap, walking in place toward the Incarnation. The baby the ass the wooden crèche the stage the microphones
body count numbers on screen, whispered voice-overs
in tall wet grass.　　　There is a mother in this picture:
her mouth moves, but she doesn't speak.　　　"After the fact."

ONCE:

"Ponder what may haue passed betvveene these tvvo diuine harts, where that Sunne and Moone so sad and eclipsed, behold one the

other: this was no doubt one of the greatest sorrowes which Christ our Lord endured, to see that meeke Doue his mother come out of the arke of her retirement, so much grieued & afflicted at the sight of him so disfigured, & enuironed with his enemies that desired to make a finall end of him . . ."

Illustration. male/female polarization as mythos

nowadays,

the sunwise mould

some goddess made

you before

you lifted,

leftward

THE EXERCISES

In order to advance, you begin the next list:

1) Pull a rope across a shower rod. Back and forth, back and forth, day after day after day. Repeat. Repeat. Repeat.

2) Continue cleaning house. House cleaning is a fine exercise.

3) List everything you remember about her when she was well.

4) Spider Walk. Walk the fingers of the affected arm as far up the wall was they will go. Mark. Facing wall and right angle. Mark. Right. Repeat. Spider Man, Spider Man, dona nobis pacem. Do whatever a spider can, at this point in time. O old Grandmother Spider, ora pro nobis

5) Consider vvhome thou cherishest, whome thou now adorest, O miserable wretch that I am, wherefore are all these riches, if I am to become so naked here? For what purpose are these deckings and braueries, I being to remaine at last so vgly and foule?

6) Avoid the sun. Avoid the scrape, the scratch. Don't wear jewelry that could scrape or scratch. Your nodes are gone; you are <u>not protected</u>. Do not cut your cuticles. Your grant of immunity has been denied, your immortality, expired.

7) Generate connective tissue from indo-european stems, until all the gaps are erased, all the expletives deleted.

8) This is the order in which things came to pass. I don't think there are any living who can remember dates, years. I doubt if very many people know what they were doing, let's say, April 10, 1970, or 1968, or any other year.

Table. The Desperate Making of Lists.

STRATEGIES		ENEMIES
1. Repression	"... there's a strange conflation of Nixon with the mother. I'm not sure that's OK.... Are we meant to feel empathy for Nixon in the way that we do for the mother? ... What does it mean to put an enemies list up against psychological strategies for dealing with cancer? It continues to be unclear to me what kind of analogy is building here. ... The documentary materials ... seem to function only as distancing devices, a strategy to escape the overwhelming pathos of the personal story. **Is the reader only an observer of tragedy here?"**	1. Daniel Schorr, CBS
2. Denial		2. Bill Cosby, actor
3. Reaction Formation		3. Jane Fonda, actress
4. Displacement		4. Sander Vanocur, NBC
5. Sublimation		5. Displacement
6. Rationalization		6. Joe Namath, New York Giants [sic], businessman, actor.
7. Isolation		7. Paul Newman, actor
8. Intellectualization		8. St. Louis Post-Dispatch
9. Projection		9. Tony Randall, actor
10. Regression		10. Barbara Streisand, actress
11. Suppression		11. Dick Gregory [handwritten]
12. Stoicism & Fatalism		12. Marvin Kalb, CBS
13. Prayer & Faith		13. John Conyers, congressman, Detroit
14. Resignation & Helplessness		14. Invasiveness and Loss of Dignity
15. St. Simian Cyborg,		15. Leonard Woodcock, UAW, Detroit

This new body-self the child won't know: he can't get "inside your skin."   "Adult child" means getting the facts but not the feel. The reader is an adult child.   I too desire the end of suffering, silences and corruption, the explanation. That Great Analogy that marks an end of mourning.

Meanwhile, the mirror awaits you without speaking:

One day you will have to   might as well look:

It will be Ugly, and it will be Red:
so absent you can't ignore so different

". . . a puckered, ugly slit — like a fiery red shirred seam."

Underneath the

Beneath

Other

a terribly offensive sight.   *flinching —*
a terribly painful thought   red

Oh may god,

My god-O   why

O my O

We didn't think that probably much would come of it; but on the other hand, something may come of it and I think it was one of those decisions that unfortunately —

Between the I and the O   Beneath the O

EYES ONLY

My mother, secretary to senators and governors, dressed to the nines, designer of her own wedding dress, paragon of elegance, Jackie look, the gloves, the hat, the thick, reptilian hide that shed gray flakes for a year, burned skin mush of flesh entire side of torso, making sure they looked symmetrical.

"Just about the time that I started to feel the true quality of the up-hill climb before me — of adjustment to a new body, a new time span, a possible early death — the pains hit."

You have back and shoulder pain, they say; insomnia; extreme sensitivity of affected touch triggers.

In spite of this, there We are, in Washington in March of '73. He in loosened tie, indicating we'd tagged along on a business trip; she looking enormously tired, but present, simulating a smile, gray putty face. A True Southern Lady never complains of her own body. I am holding a picture of President George Washington and grinning. The city is bowing around us, since everyone since has died.

March 28 — Started X-ray treatment for ispot [?]
April 18 — Saw Dr. Nickson
April 23 — Resumed treatment — chest wall
April 30 — Haldeman, Ehrlichman, Kleindienst, Dean.
May 1 — Dr. Long took X-ray
May 14 — Rose Mary Woods tells us that "Jeane Dixon tells us that
  May and June are going to be pretty bad. June may be worse than
  May. But everything will turn out fine and to be of stout heart and
  all that." [as good an explanation
*May 15 — Completed 16 treatments — Dr. Long took X-ray. I am to see
  him in 3 or 4 weeks*
May 17 — Saw Dr. Nobles. Am to see him again in 2 mo.
May 18 — Senate "Ervin" Cmte. begins televised hearings. Joe and
  Lib watch, along with everyone else, between treatments.

"So, how come he's not getting Alpo Beef Chunks Dinner?"

Q: So why did he watch the Senate hearings? Most kids his age were playing baseball or whatever.

A: Oh, he watched Henry Aaron break the record. But the family sport had always been politics — the parents met while working on the Hill, you know.

He doesn't appreciate the unbearability of it until he's an adult, of course. But he's living it then. The self ventures out and returns, developed and transformed, to the self. This is the dialectic of many happy returns. Interpolate fractured narratives, creepy concealments, lists of medications, lists of enemies, and trust in a plan. But aggression displaces everything else, twice or thrice, at least.

> MR. TALMADGE: Do you remember when we were in law school, we studied a famous principle of law that came from England and also is well known in this country, that no matter how humble a man's cottage is, that even the King of England cannot enter without his consent.
>
> MR. EHRLICHMAN [chin thrust forward, supercilious and defensive as always]: I'm afraid that has been considerably eroded over the years, has it not?
>
> MR. TALMADGE [with knowing smile]: Down in my country we still think it is a pretty legitimate principle of law. [Applause.] [Gratification. Compensation.]

Q: But how would watching the political drama unfold make that better, instead of worse?

A: Victory. To see southerners (and Democrats) — the sort of people she had worked for — destroy these slimy unprincipled bastards —

Q: What? That made up for the mother's dying?

A: Mourning is regularly the reaction to the loss of a loved person, or to the loss of some abstraction which has taken the place of one, such as one's country, liberty, an ideal, and so on.

Q: Wow. Did you write that?

A: No, Freud. Though the boy didn't know it then, of course. Nostalgia. So that couldn't be it, either.

Q: A different kind of gratification, perhaps —

A: Loss of a different memory. If done under your assurance that it is not traceable. But you tell me if you're the one who's authorizing it.

Then, later, something about *OK, so Lib's had a little too much to drink tonight,* something head-in-handed, eavesdropped. Everyone who has this story has this part.

"Going back to the analogy of cancer and the war in Vietnam, the 'medicine' we gave that country was too strong to attack only the invaders. B-52 bombers, massive artillery, napalm, and defoliants were too random and indiscriminate to hit just the 'enemy': hundreds of thousands of helpless, innocent people were killed or wounded as well. In the end, the country was destroyed by the evidence."

June 2. Saw Dr. Nobles re 2nd nodule on neck.
June 4 — Jack saw Dr. Salky + talked   — by the <u>medicine</u>."

"I don't think they even gave her a mammogram — here she had two sisters who had died of cancer, and I don't think they even gave her a mammogram. . . . Just inexcusable, really — but you know, that was back in those days . . . they just treated that so casually."

June 5 — Jack called Dr. Nobles.   Sen. Connally called Pres. Nixon: "Oh, you're gonna do more than survive, hell, you're gonna be, you're gonna come out ahead of the game" — as one might speak to the metaphorically terminal case.

SENATOR ERVIN: Well, there are two kinds of fear. There is physical fear and intellectual fear.

[A] "Mommy's sad . . . energy is less. Children are very perceptive — I don't think it's a good idea not to tell them."

[B] "It amazes me how un-perceptive kids can be, looking back. All the time I knew you, I never comprehended that your mom was ill. I think I thought that she just liked to sleep a lot or something. Finding out that she had passed away was a shock to me, but realizing that I had never even known that she was sick made it doubly so."

I

"The concept of total kill of cancer cells by combination therapy so promising in acute childhood leukemia is not so easily applied to solid tumors for reasons previously mentioned. Nevertheless, an attempt to attain a summation of therapeutic effect, a delay in development of drug resistance, and a possible diminution in toxicity by using lower doses of agents at different sites of intracellular vulnerability to achieve a more effective metabolic blockade of cell growth is very appealing in breast cancer."

II

"She won't be coming home from the hospital."

He didn't understand what his mother meant, though he knew Aunt Gin was sick.

She used the same words when her other sister went to the hospital:
"She won't be coming home."

He had grown a little by then, so a picture arose: Aunt Mary, sitting in bed, living out her years in a white room.

III

"I began by telling the President that there was a cancer growing on the Presidency and that if the cancer was not removed that the President himself would be killed by it. I also told him that it was important that this cancer be removed immediately because it was growing more deadly every day. I then gave him what I told him would be a broad overview of the situation and I would come back and fill in the details and answer any questions he might have about the matter."

Illustration. "Kids will know. . . . Even if they don't know all the details, they know something's wrong."

"She just never talked to you about her feelings?"

"Not much . . . I didn't know what to say. . . . all I could do was just be here for her . . ."

"Did she cry?"

"No. No. Once in a while, she'd get frustrated, you know. But that would pass."

DR. A: "In order to keep [family and friends] from falling apart, the woman tries to keep her chin up and have a smile plastered on her face — at a time when she herself is most defenseless and in need of support."

DR. D: "It was my particular concern with the fact that the President did not seem to understand the implications of what was going on."

"See, both of her sisters had died of cancer. And I used to lay there in bed sometime and wonder, quite selfishly I guess, how I would react if she got sick like that. And then she did."

"Was she afraid of the same thing?"

"She never said, but I'm sure she was. Had to have been. . . . I thought I would just go to pieces. But I didn't."

June 6 — Dr. Nobles recommended Dr. Fleming

June 11 — Saw Dr. Fleming — He's great — gave prescription for Drug- + will talk w/Long

June 20 — Saw Dr. Fleming. All OK. Increase medication to 3 a day.

INSERT HERE: Our Trip to St. Louis. The birds at the Zoo. The fawns at Grant's Farm. Animal tricks. The dark photos of a game at Busch Stadium. The dark glasses. Events are what kill you, exhausted by protocols. She smiles & waves, up-and-down. Smart sunny dresses. Bud Sun Hat.

July 11 — Dr. Fleming — Blood Count Low so discontinue medication 2 wks + check in with him then — Nodules decreased lately. Hair coming out at alarming rate.

July 13 — Butterfield reveals existence of taping system.

July 18 — Taping system disconnected. Silence.

July 25 — Dr. Fleming — Blood Count up — wait 2 wks (Aug. 8) and start medication 1-a-day. See him in 4 weeks. [Almost bald!] Nodules not noticeable to feel.

[A] "The loss of hair was much more devastating than I had expected it to be. . . . and you do look gray, no matter what you do with makeup, and you feel sub-human."

[B] "They feel literally deformed, and even 'freakish.' . . . may at the same time feel guilt because of the 'vanity' that her concern implies."

[C] "Ponder, what is the end of all beauty, estimation, honour, and delight of the flesh, and how little whatsoeuer thou hast enioyed hitherto, will then pleasure thee: for he who a little before pleased the eye of the beholder with his beauty and comeliness now causeth horrour & dread vnto all that looke vpon him."

[D] —Well, we have an awful lot of things then on our heads, you know, in the last couple of months, and I realize that both in numbers and in quality it almost puts us into a state of shellshock . . .

— It just makes me gag.

[E] Picture with Aunt Mary. Picture with Uncle Pete. Summer on the patio with the Wooletts. Picture with the Woodses. She was always the one who kept the family glued, the life of the party, who got along with everyone, made sure everyone got along, even the fractious Fords. She was making sure she saw everyone again. All the Dyersburg folks, at least, everyone all along again. Genealogical repair.

[F] Metastasis ≠ stasis. I was trying to hold my own in the new parochial school, uniformed, uninformed, when the glass in the transom over our classroom door exploded, for no apparent reason, on a calm, clear day. I was sitting next to it; no one was hurt, no one could explain. One doesn't talk about such things.

[G] Well, I think we ought to let him hang there.
Let him twist slowly, slowly in the wind.

[H]

[I] This is a story that has to be told, by me.

I remember my ideas of all these people.

Your life amounts to, if you're not famous

dove coo, column break

As told to.

I can more easily think of

History, uses childhood for myth

what would you do with the past?

Memories go backward from ending

Her, before a mother borne

"A majority of viewers responded by saying they were 'tired of Watergate.'" We kept watching as though we couldn't help it.

Aug. 23 — Saw Dr. Fleming — Blood Count OK. Continue 1-a-day.

Sept. 27 — Saw Dr. Fleming — Blood Count a bit lower (white) but OK. Continue 1-a day. See him in 3 wks. Nodule on Rt. noticeable to feel but he "isn't worried."

Oct. 20, 1973 — "Saturday Night Massacre."

Oct. 22 — Saw Dr. Fleming. Blood Count OK + R. nodule "seems even a bit smaller" — Come back in 4 wks. Hair beginning to grow back. Eyes giving a bit of trouble, esp. left — To see Dr. Holmes 11/1

Nov. 1 — Saw Dr. Holmes — No change in glasses needed. Gave Drops for "allergy" —

Nov. 6 — Saw Dr. Dunaway again re rash — Another medication —

Nov. 7 — Saw Dr. Porter re cough + Laryngitis — He increased Dr. Dunaway's medication!

> ". . . the cancer that it was, you know, advanced, and that — she cried and she said, I'm only sorry — she said — I won't get to see him grow up."
>
> "She said that, huh?"
>
> "Yeah."
>
> "Me too."

I tacked a lurid blacklight poster to my closet door: a cartoon Nixon, restraining growling hounds with faces like Haldeman's, Ehrlichman's, Dean's, Magruder's — a nightmare poster, really. An augury.

Watergate helped me concentrate, like baseball. Thank you, Henry Aaron. Thank you, Sam Dash.

"DEEP SIX" THE BRIEFCASE
SHRED THE BODY OF

This experience has taught me how fast things can "come on" — said
matter-of-factly — almost offhandedly, as one would open a letter,
with an aside. *Án Cailleach*, the *Mor-Ríoghain*, a cloud of black crows
raising Hel as they fly home to roost in midtown: Grand Mother, Old
Crow. Does her dying echo things' falling apart, or coming home to
roost?

> *— and should the bad times*
> *come, it is hard to make decisions.*

the agencyless, choiceless
position of the mother

> *— Joe, Sugar, don't confuse your*
> *readers so. Why don't you just come*
> *right out and say what you <u>mean</u>?*

"I started to have nightmares . . . about Watergate. I felt
that the institutions were being abused, and that in a very
personal sense, I was being abused."

> blackwhat? . . . Waterloo?

Our Gardens — *1974*

May 5, 1974 — As we are just now starting a "log" of this year's gar-
dening efforts, I will have to give a resumé of what has already been
done —

Jack planted lettuce (
last fall which he cultivated in early spring, first part of April. Also planted
more lettuce (   ) and red radishes
(SPARKLER). We've had lettuce + radishes since about April 15.
Early April he planted squash plants.

May 5 — At Penal Farm, Joe planted corn — Jack planted cantalope +
onions.

> planted, nor picked nor pulled.

April 11, 1974

Jack, dear heart —

This experience has taught me how fast things can "come on" — and should the bad times come, it is hard to make decisions. I've left a "Final Request" note with my will + this will elaborate on that, hopefully to make things easier for you.

I would like to be buried in Dyersburg and hope Frances will sell us a one-grave plot next to Gin. (If she balks at sell, but will let us have it, Ok, and you can send her a bond or something) Uncle Bill will call + ask for you, I feel sure. I'd like this done ahead of time so there won't be any stalling when it is needed immediately.

If this doesn't work out, I would like to be buried in the Ford lot in the Old Cemetery. Ask Uncle Bill how this is done.

If neither of these places is available, then don't bury me in Dyersburg. If I can't be in a family plot, then Memphis Jackson, wherever you choose —

Illustration

If Dyersburg, just call J.W. Curry + Son and they will come and get one. You, or Uncle Bill, or both, or somebody, will have to go to Curry's to make arrangements. Please don't get an expensive casket, I liked the lovely wooden one Martha T. had. Curry will call Fr. Fisher + arrange Mass. Morning is the best time – 10 or 11. Uncle Bill will know who to get for Pall Bearers.

You'll have to take some clothes for me – Some of the girls I like can help you decide. I want my wedding band on and the heart forget-me-not pearl pen. Also I'm sure I'll need the grey wig –

I hope Frances + Jud can come when the chips are down. They could be helpful in a day-or nite duty situation. Also I'd like her to dispose of my clothes + costume jewelry, etc. with your agreement.

My prosthesis I'd like to offer to the Cancer Soc. as it could sure help someone. Phyllis could do this for you. The size is on the Bra. I love you –

I'd like a tombstone like Mother's + Daddy's.

Illustration. True Southern Lady. poise, when it's all
one has at last.

She never left Dyersburg.	From the first.
There was no day + nite.	There was no family at
last. it's all one has	This duty

"4 of 8 planets were stationary — that makes things happen in a big way. This is what we were all wondering about during Watergate. . . . Mars through 12th house . . . outer planets reversal . . . brings things into consciousness. . . . 'well,' we said, 'all their secrets will come out ! . . .'"

WOULD-BE GRAVE GOODS. Did I mention he said she never told him about the letter?

"She kept going, just like always," ▄▄ says. Her date book for 1974 has all the relatives' birthdays, car inspection deadlines, even beyond the day of her ▄▄▄▄. One can even imagine what will happen next. Haldeman can't stop taking notes; Dean can't not remember everything.

"Things are going to change now. And they're going to change, and, and — "

" — and I thought it was time that everybody start thinking about telling the truth."

I

"She won't be coming home from the hospital." Now his father says it, of his mother, this time.

II

[I then gave him what I told him would be a broad overview of the situation and I would come back and fill in the details and answer any questions he might have about the matter.]

III

"After Inouye's questioning, a voice is heard saying 'Boy, what a liar.' Inouye denies it was his voice."

ORDERED TO LIE ON THE TABLE
AND TO BE PRINTED

MRS. G — — : Well, the cancer didn't kill her, the <u>chemo</u> killed her.

MR. FRIEDMAN: I'm sorry, ma'am, but the President has made his decision.

A VOICE FROM THE AUDIENCE: Why isn't the President being impeached for war crimes? Aren't lives more important than tapes?

MR. HARRINGTON (Kan.): Yes, but the squirrels in the yard didn't seem to care what went on in the House. I hold that against them, though we didn't care about them either, I'm sure. But did I watch them, too? Things go on without you, whether you watch them or not, nuts hid, eggs planted.

MR. HESS: I must admit, I haven't liked wallowing in this filth. I feel unclean even listening. . . . as I leave you, I'm distressed and I'm burned out and I salute you for performing a useful though distressing service, and I wish you fortitude and a strong stomach.

MR. HARRINGTON (Tenn.): But there toward the end . . . incontinence . . . [grimaces and shakes head]

MR. DOWNIE: . . . We felt small. . . . Most of us were dysfunctional the night . . . It was hard. . . . at the time it was dirty. People weren't sleeping, people weren't showering . . . it was difficult to figure out what was going on . . .

MR. HARRINGTON (Kan.): . . . Yet <u>we</u> didn't camp out in the lounge like the other animals. We only dropped in for our nightly visit after dinner at Morrison's Cafeteria.

MR. HARRINGTON (Tenn.): Well, I had to work — I had to support you. . . .

A VOICE FROM THE AUDIENCE: How you must have felt! —

MR. HARRINGTON (Kan.): I often had fried haddock with a side of black-eyed peas. Or perhaps carrot-and-raisin salad. I had ceased drinking chocolate milk at this point in time.

A SECOND VOICE: — Verily, a blunt instrument!

MR. NIXON [sighs audibly]: It's all such a bunch of Goddamn dirty shit.

Illustration. On the Day of Ragnarök,
seven evil kings were killed   the End

PISCES (Feb. 19–March 20): Continue imposing a form. In elegy, I is always the subject, but a narrative opens outward, thereby providing an order. Even a list. Even a pattern of stars. Find the two fishes, swimming against each other in a circle. What is the story behind it? Answer by pasting the scraps.

June 15, 1974 — Rose Kushner discovers a small lump in her left breast.

"This I am not really definite on. The words I can remember from it are 'Joe's,' 'Stone crab.'" : a summer sign. Hers.

You really do have to think long term: the same in this universe and a universe to come: in the myriad kalpas of gigabytes of worlds: and later I have to go pick up some milk. It's just that I don't especially like all those creatures in the Cambrian shale, and I don't appreciate the idea of cutesy sea otters and cerulean warblers dropping dead to make way for microorganisms and bivalves and people like me. The something there is that doesn't love a life loves Life. What was your face before you were born? It's right there in the fossil record. Endless, sickening iterations of nightmares led to me. Where is the black milk. We led too. In this change in the earth to come, the Republic will endure.

[and if I go through with this, I won't end up like her — that is the promise of the incantation —]

HARRINGTON, ELIZABETH P. AGE 58   3593 Gennessee St.
HARRINGTON, ELIZABETH P. AGE 53   3993 Genasee St.
HARRINGTON, ELIZABETH P. AGE 58   3593 Tennessee St.
HARRINGTON, ELIZABETH P. AGE 52   3393 Genessee St.
HARRINGTON, ELIZABETH P. AGE 52   3593 Tennesee St.

PORTABLE CHEST: shows the heart within normal limits

Flame before glass reflects
flames inside ribcage
Heart immolate
Broken hearth rages

Find "your voice" — puff
combustion
flick-lit smoke

Why do you think
they call us ghosts?
Who's to say the mouse
isn't?   in pulses,

intervals,

II. RESIGNATION

SENSITIVE
MATERIAL

**Handle As
Codeword
Material**

**Exdis
No Disem**

"That dealt with some sort of a drug and a girl in a hospital.
That is all I can tell you about."

When her hospital file was recovered, I said
"Look! it starts with my birth. . . ."

HARRINGTON, ELIZABETHP Date Admitted: 06/27/74
Breast Carcinoma   Code: 174

Hour: 1:00 Sex: F Age: 52 Race: W
How admitted: Stretcher
Previous Illnesses: Mastectomy 72. Pneumonia April 74
Valuables: none
Dietary Habits: Reg
Bowel and/or Bladder: Reg Bowel. incontinent
                              of urine @ times
States she started having dizzy spells 3 4 days ago Color pale
Appears to be very weak

"Plumbers" jury sworn in, avg. age 42. Includes one housewife.

6/28 > wk of less hx of marked weakness dizziness + palpitations on
standing. Dyspnea upon standing. Has pulse 120+ lying, > 160 sit-
ting w/ loss of pulse BP 75/0 lying.
          Hypovolemia Acute + severe
          Prob. Hemorrhagic cystitis 2° meds

CONSTITUTIONAL CRISIS

Perhaps this isn't an analogy . . . perhaps it is the record of a person's
death. Or a history coming apart. A descent into the underworld,
where Ulasewicz taped a key to the bottom of the locker. Presenting
skullduggery; oncology astrology indicated.

"some of the concepts were mind-boggling and the charts were in code names . . ."

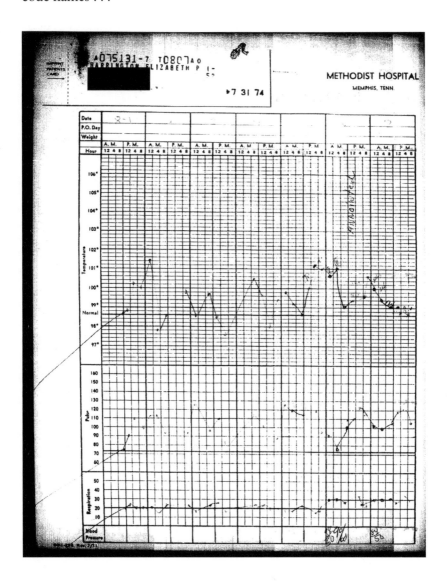

[1 November 2009   "No wonder
you feel overwhelmed . . . how can you understand a
void?"]

Ruby 1   Ruby 2   Crystal
Haldeman = "The Brush"
Mitchell = "The Pipe"
Hunt = "The Writer"

29 June — tremors AM — will cath — [illegible]

"fatigue, restlessness, frustration and recrimination"

8:30 — States short of breath — pale.
            Side Rails ↑ Bed in semi-fowler's position —

        ("maybe a scenario has been worked out in advance")

30 June — Continues with dyspnea — ↓ course

"feels confused and trapped, startled by the evidence . . . but
        frightened by the consequences."

eruption

            attacked,

"Things have gotten out of hand, but I'm afraid they're going to get
worse."
            "every major substantive part . . .
violated, abused and undermined"

— the violence, the violation . . . The pocket poet-doctor
snoop must open you up to set things straight or no body
will
— OK, but what's your point? You seem a little bit too angry
to write this.

Deep wind peace of the ringing chime to you.

The blood has been prepared. The family brings new blood.
And what if excess of blood bedeviled them till they lied

A mottledy rabbit hunkered in mottledy sycamore leaves,
tucked inside-under the leafless climbing rose.

All together, this comes down to: to come back, to come on,

ORDERED TO LIE

ON THE TABLE

TO BE PRINTED

1. Watership Down

2. Jaws

JUL 1 1974

1:30 — AM care given. Pt. upset at this time because did not
believe she received adequate care — linens changed but pt.
very dispirited. IV has been infusing well all day.

HEAD AND NECK: swelling   ↑ venous filling
THORAX AND LUNGS, INCLUDING BREASTS: left
breast absent   B[reath]. S[ounds]. n[i]l.

Kalmbach waits in vain for sympathy or encouragement.

[illegible]

↑ NRBC — probable marrow in-
volvement follow the

JUL 2 Pt. spiked Temp to 101.5° @ 2 pm c ↓ B.P.
extrapleural fluid

+ perhaps

2:00 — Shortness of breath on exertion. Seems very de-
pressed.

[ah — & surely <u>this</u> is the <u>personal</u>
very
ttruth of the matter!]

Q: Yes — where are <u>you</u> in all this? Where is Joe?
A: I'm sorry, my mind is not a tape recorder. I do not trust this
talking form. I do not trust this tape recorder. . . . Now make
it talk back.

6:00 — Appears to have slept well at short intervals. O_2

11:00 — How could he not have known? He monitored So-
viet missile activity, table settings, Rose Garden plantings,
paperclips. He listens in. He lies and lowers. He's every-
where.

VOIDING

avoiding

withhold information

deny any inference

re: the Matter — the "operation"

Necessity of covert entry

as if the missing —

4 July — no change — progressive disease —

8:00 — self-evident —

5 July 74 — CHEST, PORTABLE AP: pleural thickening entire left
hemithorax laterally. The heart
continues to be within
normal limits.

6 July — distended

staring into voids too long? :

to examine files

no, "this is about saying goodbye → this is about moving on."

SENATOR BAKER: Before you do, let me reiterate, the focus of my in-
quiry is on what did the President know —
MR. DEAN: As I say, this agenda went directly to the President.
SENATOR BAKER [continuing]: And when did he know it.
MR. DEAN: That is correct.

7/7 12:00 — reading. no complaints; each single one of
memories and expectations . . . brought up and hyper-
cathected,

10p. Reg diet taken ~~well~~ fair
      Color pale
      Rails up

1. All the President's Men
2. The Gulag Archipelago
3. Alive

        reading <u>what</u>? (as though the evidence made any difference
now)

7/9 12:30 — BP 104/66, resp 24, pul 88, temp. 97, depressed

7/10 — 8 tapes released by House panel

7/11 — Unchanged. Back on chemotherapy.

1:30 — sprits improved. Somewhat cheerful today. States *I'm hungry
& food tastes good!* Ate well regular diet.

ST. URISED: Ora pro nobis.
ST. LASIX: Ora pro nobis.
ST. CYTOXAN: Ora pro nobis.
ST. METHOTREXATE: Ora pro nobis.

Mitchell's failing memory (or "stone-walling")
W.H. admits withholding cover-up tape
7/12 — x-ray shows no appreciable change.
                        Dyspnea ↓.
        Better spirits.

over 4,000 pages +

"growing cynicism and apathy" &

~~TAPE ERASURE~~

She sounds so <u>southern</u> — like Blanche DuBois, almost.
broken patio tiles w/grass growing between & nothing to do
house hearings   waiting for shoes to drop and drop   what
is <u>your</u> smoking gun?   who shot   Wait.

                              Gap hum like 18.5 min.
                              signals from Pluto >

                              Was there a "Q"? If so,
                              Paul burned it.

"Well, I'd cut the loss fast. I'd cut it fast. If we're going to do it, I'd cut
it fast."

9:00 — States she doesn't feel she can do without O_2 as yet.
        Seems some stronger —

10 pm Color fair
        tonight   fluids
      Up on side   color

              Rails

JUL 22 1974

No complaints

8:30   used.
                                 color
                                 amt.

7/23   WBC = 600
        Will continue present RX
        CIA chemo

        dinner parties   industrialists

final report   probing his state of mind — nurse's code
burglary of subject's privacy for missing being

JUL 24 1974 —

        Specimen from

                "nonlegal" investigations unit

8–0 Court orders W.H. surrender tapes; Nixon yields.

                Silver ↑

        "agonized" or "agonizing"
        "air of saddened defeatism"

Q: And the family? The father to son, anyway?
A: You don't know what the word "surreptitious" means?

7/27   Will not attempt to Rx if   . Continues —
        [illegible]
        debates wording.   [She is making me do this.]

Rose Kushner begins assembling notes for a draft of the book *Breast Cancer* "[b]etween sessions of the House Judiciary Committee's impeachment hearings."

"swollen with power"   slow deterioration

nightly drives to midtown, humid windows down, continuous cicada soundtrack, parking garage, elevator, nurses' station, hall, room smell, repeat, with regional variations, for everyone doing this same trip this same night, as words over radio, TV

"We're all emotionally drained and physically drained, too. But we're doing it because we think we have a duty to do it."

7/28
        Nupercainal
                green liquid   dis-
        tended

one doesn't write such things in a poem
        therefore: This is not a poem.

        whereupon everything that was touched
        was corroded

        Cmte. approves first article 27–11
        Rm. 2141 Rayburn Bldg.

"moved swiftly and with an air of detached fatalism"
"bowing to the obvious" medicalized lexicon

        what is it what it is   [I am making her]

history becomes fate when
it's over with

no more disjunct
than this world

A gateway timeout occurred
The server   /   is unreachable

History abounds
a keeling curve
this starts to be how it gets
to keening

love filters   :   red void

Molly's mussels live-o
while she dies-o —
that's the point, see?
                          A space
is a character too

One remembers that, if not what

The space is more historical
than the stars

JUL 29 1974 — [illegible]

Nixon described as stoical and self-controlled
                    Foley reported draining well.

        [as though he were about to run on his sword . . .]

(abuse of power violation of oath) secret police   Santiago

doing such things to a child. Adults, to other adults replicate
Order

7/30 — W.H. surrenders first set of subpoenaed tapes to Sirica

                            you can't vanish without a trace, but you
                                            can disap-
                        pear,   be

"The new cases of breast cancer every year would fill Yan-
        kee Stadium . . . in ten years of the Vietnam War,
        310,000 women have died from cancer of the breast"

Small decubitis

Irrigated happened s/ 30 cc

to the painful Larger when instilling

UNITY

31 July — progressive   —   and Progress

reconcile opposites, find your true self, plaintiff made whole,
        a chart, a rhyme-scheme, spell, court, spiel — the Un-
        ion un-violated — Universal Identity in an Absolute
        Idea — a constellation of systemic explanation

        primarily a matter of nursing care — no

Q: Where is "the smoking pistol"?
A: Room too full of smoke

Judiciary Cmte approves article 3 21–17; votes down articles 3 and
4 — "political overkill"; ends deliberations.

> "I wish she'd written something down for me."
>
> "I wish she had, too. I guess she didn't know what to say. I
> wouldn't. . . . What can you say? There are so many things
> you want to say, and — you know, how do you pick 'em
> out? How do you decide what to put down?"

[plong plong of mantle clock can be heard in background at this
point on tape, followed by shredding of narrative options in Washing-
ton, Saigon, Memphis, elsewhere]

"I did make the assumption that he did know but he did not say that
he did know but he did not say that he was aware of the specifics and
never did say that to me at any time."

AUG 2 1974

12 AM B/P 84/
4 AM Bp /52 [?]
5 Am — Has not
     no
     + initiated
10:30 — Bp 92/60
     2p Remains in   most all   except
     for very brief period   —
     discarded by
     regarding collection
     discrepancies on transcripts

President administered

measures exhausted

altered memos — bluish w/thick white sediments.

Gather hence a great feare and terrour, calling to mind the insup-
portable paines and trauailes that they body and soule are to endure
in the houre of death, and withal a liuely desire neuer more to forget
the same whilest thou liuest.

DEMEROL: Dona nobis pacem

THORAZINE: Dona nobis p.r.n. restlessness

---

how can anyone be permitted to feel this
1. tinker, tailor, soldier, spy

avoid loss of emoluments
paralysis
instability

drought

(all of this is <u>true history</u> — isn't that enough?
since whatever you're feeling
stays invisible in you no matter how many words without)

5 Aug — Deteriorating more rapidly —

Cytoxan tab Refused. (Medication discarded after pt. tried to swal-
low tab. coughing + tab fell from mouth 3 x's).

[— ed. note: this is why she couldn't receive the Sacrament b/c
she couldn't swallow anything.]

[— ed. note: In a fugue, all of the various themes come to-
gether in the end. This movement provides the reso-
lution it creates the expectation of, where the b-d
comes back removed, where the graft doesn't take
revisions as stints or stunts   incisions
ectomies   otomies   emotes

R22 — turned 66% impeachment

Nixon summons lawyer, aides, speech writers, family
The News tells us the end is near — vigil before TV to see it
thru as though someone were dying

Bp 85/50 101.2   Respiration
                    smoking

         2.) [Withdrawn. Privacy.]

8/6 — 1.) No Emog w. House

NATIONAL NIGHTMARE

6 AM — very difficult for pt. to swallow — followed by seize of
    coughing. Tongue and inside of mouth coated blue from
    Urised, a terrible, deep midnight blue. This is the last time I
    saw her; I remember being peeved at her; she seemed so out
    of it.   "It's JOE," I said, too loud.
    I know who you are, she said.

    Aggression toward the dying mother? — I'm not sure that's
    OK. Not at all OK.

6:45 — Dozing and apparently resting @ present. Condition remains
    Critical — Advise Last Rites!

9:10 — quiet — Wants to be "let alone" —

11:00 — asleep   quiet
                                    still

respiration of sky
moisture of sheets:
dying   not so private
as everyone supposed she
says to me

the most poletical subject —
don't lie —   how come —
click   cut   paste precise
poet   surgeon   son

                                        & luckier

                          l ck

                                              ck

_____

". . . without going into the details — don't, don't lie to them to the
extent to say there is no involvement, but just say this is a comedy of
errors, without getting into it . . . and [unintelligible] don't go any fur-
ther into this case period!"
_____

12:00 — B.p. 88/50   Moans + grunts on being turned — does
     not help self very well today —

She died on the same day Nixon announced his resignation;
     how she would've loved to have seen that.

8:30 — Husband & son [illegible]
10:30 — Semi-Comotose???
11:00 — "how perplexed and troubled thou vvilt be in that
traunce & agony of death . . ."

                         great difficulty

     We watched his speech in the Dyersburg Holiday
Inn, where we stayed on the eve of the funeral.

Nixon in "bargaining stage" nearly excised remiss

edematous. Is alert — answers when spoken too. Due to SOB,
     takes great effort to talk. Timing a coincidence

          "there was an air of relief, almost giddiness, through-
          out the House."

               Moans and wimpers

"And now a wave of melancholy tranquility settles over
Thebes."

                    — Moving legs up + down.

     Next day, we made it through the Mass. Mrs. Lenahan, my
teacher, was very kind. People kept calling and calling. Covered
dishes came to our house with them.

                                        Turning
                              head side to side.

vows to see process run its course

Goldwater and Senate Republicans c̄ Nixon to break news.

Reality-testing demands

No one tells her she can quit

      Responds to questions. Says, "I can understand the English language, it's my mother tongue. [Laughter.]"

"I don't know what they can do to pull it out."

dollar ↓   gold ↑

The kids didn't know what to say. Gov. Dunn was "extremely disappointed." p.o. 2 Turned and positioned. Again offered pt. oral intake

    and pt refused to open mouth. Just says *NO*.

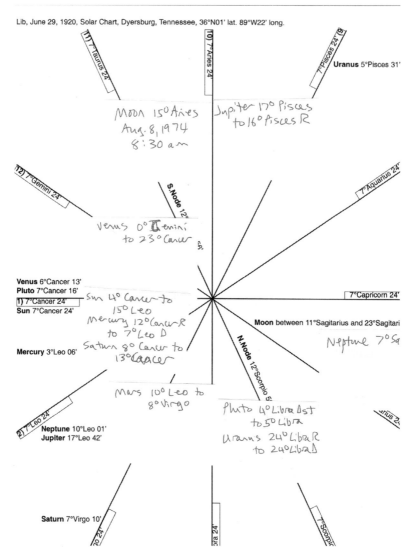

Illustration. Early diagram of the onset of the apparition of   the coming of death.

---

on September the 12th of 1964.

H. You've got a helluva memory, man, you know that?

C. Yeah, because every time that I can remember things there was a coup on, an attempt, on the 13th of that month.

H. It has nothing to do with astrological signs and concatenations. Well, when you were back for that long session, you posed an interesting thought yesterday on something that sounded entirely logical to me. I'd never heard it espoused before, and it had to do with your thoughts that the Catholicism of the then President was a factor.

Illustration.   Early diagram of the onset of the appa-

rition of   the coming of death.

4:20 — hyperventilating and groaning — acted as if she were having a [illegible].

5 am — Pt. appears to be **fighting or dreaming**. Will open eyes upon [illegible] her **Elizabeth** but does not respond

> Maybe that was when the kids at school started treating
> me better. I was on the football team that fall.

6:45 — Husband called via phone to inform him of change in condition — Condition Critical

7:15 — Lt. hand cold —   grunting   @int.   —
    shallow   cyanotic

8:00 — Husband Notified p telephone condition of pt. Neyther was there any who woold go & aduertise the most Blessed Virgin of the extreme need & nakedness of her beloued Sonne, that she might with speed come to couer him with her veile, who so often had wrapped him in cloths when he was a child.

8:35 a.m. Asked to see patient by nurses as vital signs have ceased. She is without spont. vital signs. Pupils are dilated + fixed.
    1.) Death. from pulmonary metastasis of breast

ca. 10:00 p.m. — Nixon announces resignation, effective T noon; Joe Harrington and Marguerite P. watch on TV in Dyersburg, Tenn. He tells her not to smoke or she'll die. Writing all this was supposed to make him feel better, to solve the semantic puzzle, remedy the ontic ache. We should be able to vote on the road to recovery in real time — reality-testing t.v. Be a "Survivor." Do something other than merely watch them enact what has already transpired.

> "against every instinct in my body."

Later that morning: When we came off the elevator onto the floor, we started down the hallway, past the nurses' station, when one of the nurses, an African-American woman maybe in her 30s, intercepted us. Her face in real pain, upturned slightly, she said, "Mr. Harrington? I'm sorry; she's gone." He grimaced jerkily and made to snap his fingers, like he did when he remembered something he'd left at home. "Oh! I wanted to be there!" he said. Where? He went away to take care of the body. The Disposition. She stayed with me in the (now-empty) waiting room. She stared out the window, near to tears. Southern black women taking care of southern white boys (again). "Do you want to cry?" I did not. "I guess it hasn't sunk in yet," we agreed. Motherless child: come lord jesus.   I can't know what she feels.   I don't know what
he feels.   I just feel   for them.

THE WHITE HOUSE

WASHINGTON

1/2/73

TO: John Dean

FROM: Charles Colson

Now what the hell do I do?

8-7-74 [sic]   1) Discharge body to morgue

2) Notify proper individuals.

3) Heaven not at all like Yankee Stadium.

8-9-74 Richard Nixon wakes up in the morning.

11:35 a.m. — "Dear Mr. Secretary,
I hereby resign the office of President of the United States.

Sincerely,

Richard Nixon"

"au revoir"

---

physical death no metaphor
to transport you over or down river

physical fear of intellectual fear
mother   not
all the things   ings happening
at once would be an

afterwards

an afterword   an Over & Out.

    The Republic will survive   mutation
[they "didn't get all of it out"]

          paralysis

The Dead will dead

       they may be

pyrrhic

meta-static

grown up

12:03 p.m. — Ford takes oath.

   2) Nixon family flees Saigon.

   3) "bind up the internal wounds"

   3) long national nightmare declared over.

   4) "The year 1974 has rightly been called the
   turning point for breast cancer awareness in
   the United States."

   5) Constitution healthy.

   6) A list will continue running in the
      background.

"Nobody will ever write a book, probably, about my mother.
Well, I guess all of you would say this about your mother:
My mother was a saint."

The Classical Unities. The Dénouement.

The phone rang constantly. Finally, I began picking up the receiver
and immediately replacing it on the switch hook. This had the effect
of terminating the incoming call as soon as it had been initiated.

NO.

AUGUST 8

Mon. **1938**. *Gloom, gloom, gloom!*
What to do.

Illustration.

& life meanwhile goes on, on pg. 17:

over here

the ad for "Chinatown"

the ad for "Steak n' Stuff"

She also leaves a daughter, Miss Callie McDonald, and three sons, Harold McDonald III, David McDonald and Steven McDonald, all of the home, and her mother, Mrs. Don Heiden of Cornwells Heights, Pa.

Mrs. J. F. Harrington

Mrs. Elizabeth Peoples Harrington, 54, of ███████ ███████ wife of ███ Harrington and former executive secretary to Sen. Albert Gore, died yesterday at Methodist Hospital.

Mrs. Harrington served as Gore's secretary in his Washington and Memphis offices.

Mass will be said at 1 p.m. today at Holy Angels Catholic Church in Dyersburg, Tenn., with burial in Fairview Cemetery there. Curry Funeral Home of Dyersburg has charge.

She also leaves a son, Joseph Harrington of Memphis.

Mrs. Mattie Andereck

War 1
He
S. Tu
his p
Jame
and a
Tune

W
Will
1038
died
St. Jo
Gra
at 10
tende
Mario
al Ho
has ch
He
Willey
ter, M
Evans
grand

Mrs.

Mrs
of Br
Georg
died
Abrah
York.
a.m.
Chapel

Well, you can see whether the subject matches the verb, the moon transiting the sun in Pisces semisextile — unconscious connection — and that sort of thing, but to know what the content is means "Not Gone." I think you don't read it well enough to retain it in your mind as to something about Saturn and Pluto conjunct (or is it "conjoined"? I don't remember whether he changed "to" or a "by" or what it was). And so, to that plutonian shore I came, having failed to recognize instructions for closing the womb.

Or more precisely "Do not be dead."

December 9, 1961

Dear Mary Sugg —

Words are very inadequate to try to express our grief — or to try to offer consolation. But Jack and I do want you to know you and the rest of the family are in our thoughts and prayers. We have lost someone very dear to us, too, and hope there is consolation in knowing that your grief is shared. Miss Bessie Lee gave so much pleasure to so many people — and will be long remembered and loved for her many kindnesses. I feel that my life is richer for having known her and know all my family feel the same.

May God be with you and comfort you in this great and untimely loss.

Our love,

Lib and Jack

(A) "I hear some men say, 'I've forgotten what she looked like.' Not <u>me</u>."

(B) "Never. Never, her name was never mentioned again . . . It sort of became like she had never existed."

(A) "Washington . . . willing, and almost eager to forget."

(B) "These individuals are never quite sure of who died and whom they are missing — whether it is the idealized mom of the childhood or a real person."

GOD DAMN GOD DAMN GOD

—Things come up and on o yes they are
     a bunch of dirty squalid rotten shit
—What? That's IT? The mother dies, and the country
    (Today We Know) only got worse. That's the ending?
    That's all you can say for yourself? Where's the redemption
    in <u>that</u>? The Revelation? The positive example of survival
    and endurance?
—Tragedy means you can only observe,
     static, while everything changed.
— Senator, that is just a thing that is not true and it is a
    tragic thing that anybody could even think that it might be
    true.

Q: Is it not enough just to write down the story?

A: The Tomb of the Unknown Woman. Under Eve's.

my mother lives under the ground
so I am drawn to that country

still air cools   water trickles black
roots tower   down   in her house

up here a sky   never whole
buoys around   light of the moon

    I could spend half a year
down where she always lives

A white cockatoo turns around and around in circles in the dirt, and I can't understand why. Then there are four white cockatoos, turning a wheel, like the pet parrots of Fortuna. Then she's waving us all into the biergarten, and everything brightens and blurs, and that's the last I see of her. After that, I can only make out washed-out images

of flowering shrubs.

Notes

Uncited quotations in body text come from first-person sources or are paraphrases of several secondary sources; some of these are inside quotation marks. Not all cited quotations are in quotation marks.

The abbreviation SSC refers to United States Congress, Senate Select Committee on Presidential Campaign Activities, *Presidential Campaign Activities of 1972: Watergate and Related Activities*. 93rd Congress, 1st and 2nd sess. 26 vols. (Washington: GPO, 1973–74).

I. INVESTIGATION

page 5

"Betty Ford's breast cancer": Ellen Leopold, *A Darker Ribbon: Breast Cancer, Women, and Their Doctors in the Twentieth Century* (Boston: Beacon Press, 1999), p. 232.

"Scare the shit out of them": Richard Nixon, on White House tape, Aug. 3, 1972.

page 6

"Like all outstanding anniversaries": Rose Kushner, *Alternatives* (Cambridge, Mass.: The Kensington Press, 1984), p. 1.

"It depends on who is telling the story": as "to who looks like the White Knight and who looks like the Black Knight, of course." Testimony of John Mitchell to the Senate Select Committee on Watergate, Tuesday, July 10, 1973. SSC, bk. 4, p. 1612.

page 7

"*stomach tightening*," etc.: Reactions to learning of diagnosis of malignant breast cancer. See esp. Betty Rollin, *First, You Cry* (Philadelphia: J. B. Lippincott Company, 1976), p. 38.

"I think all three of us were appalled": Testimony of Jeb Stuart Magruder before the Senate Select Committee, Thursday, June 14, 1973. SSC, bk. 2, p. 788.

"Creating a story out of the fragments": Lynn Davidman, describing the notion of "biographical disruption and repair," in *Motherloss* (Berkeley, Calif.: Univ. of California Press, 2000), p. 47.

"That's why a list is in order": "If the body of the text has suffering at its root, then language will take a fragmented, torn-apart form, as if it too is suffering."

Kristin Prevallet, *I, Afterlife: Essay in Mourning Time* (Athens, Ohio: Essay Press, 2007), p. 50.

page 8

"whisked away under cover of darkness": Leopold, pp. 237-38. "Well, the scriptures say that men love darkness rather than light because of the deeds of evil. Somebody must have covered up something back in the scripture days to quote that. [Laughter.]" Sen. Sam Ervin, Chair of the Senate Select Committee, during Magruder's testimony. SSC, bk. 2, p. 860.

"I did know absolutely nothing": that would "implicate Mr. Mitchell [former Atty. Gen. and Chair of Committee to Re-Elect the President]." Sally J. Harmony, G. Gordon Liddy's secretary, testimony before the Senate Select Committee, Tuesday, June 5, 1973. SSC, bk. 2, p. 468.

page 9

"operation and irradiation": W. J. Burdette, "Surgical Therapy for Primary Mammary Cancer." *Breast Cancer: A Challenging Problem*, ed. M.L. Griem et al. *Recent Results in Cancer Research 42* (New York: Springer-Verlag, 1973), p. 97. Copyrighted © material from this volume used with kind permission of Springer Science+Business Media.

"oral history on paper": This paradox occurs in Lyn Hejinian, *My Life* (Los Angeles: Sun and Moon Press, 1987), p. 8.

"We are going to use any means": Richard Nixon on White House tape, July 1, 1971.

page 10

"the famous fingers": Magruder testimony, SSC, bk. 2, pp. 796–97. "The FBI struck pay dirt when . . . a Miami photographer . . . told agents that a week before the break-in, a man . . . had come to his store . . . [with] two rolls of exposed 35 millimeter film that he wanted developed immediately and printed in eight-by-ten enlargements. . . . [T]hey were photographs of documents, most of which had an emblem and 'Chairman, Democratic National Committee' printed on them. The documents were photographed against a background of shag carpeting. Hands in clear gloves held down the corners of each document." Mark Felt and John O'Connor, *A G-Man's Life: The FBI, Being "Deep Throat," and the Struggle for Honor in Washington* (New York: PublicAffairs, 2006), p. 204.

"I do not mind telling you any fact that is true": "Mr. DEAN [conferring with counsel]. He just said, which was quite accurate, I do not mind telling you any fact that is true. [Laughter.] // Senator BAKER. I would say that was a very lawyer-like piece of advice. [Laughter.]" SSC, bk. 4, p. 1480.

"struggle to speak themselves into existence": kari edwards, "NARRATIVE/
IDENTITY." Narrativity 3 (n.d.) http://www.sfsu.edu/~poetry/narrativity/
issue_three/edwards.html.
Accessed 2 July 2010.
"a frustration and a feeling": Magruder's testimony, SSC, bk. 2, p. 854.

page 11
"It's as if the file is missing": "Sid," one of Davidman's respondents, in reference
to lack of memories of his mother. *Motherloss*, p. 102.

page 12
"believe that the proper thing ever": Surgically altered statement of Hon. Delbert
L. Latta, United States Congress, House Judiciary Committee, *Debate on
Articles of Impeachment*, 93rd Congress, 2nd sess. H. Res. 803 (Washington:
GPO, 1974), pp. 114–15.
"The code words": John Mitchell, testimony to Senate Select Committee,
characterizing G. Gordon Liddy's "Gemstone" operation. Tuesday, July
10, 1973. SSC, bk. 4, p. 1610. "I think that we all had an innate fear
that during the campaign that they might be revealed." SSC, bk. 4,
p. 1625.

page 13
"a pathetic puff of lambswool": Audre Lorde's description of the temporary
"falsie" distributed to new "mastectomies" by the American Cancer Society's
Reach to Recovery program. In *The Cancer Journals* (San Francisco: aunt lute
books, 1980), p. 59.
"prevents a woman": Lorde, p. 57.
"We didn't want Reach to Recovery to become a crutch": A representative of the
program, quoted in Kushner, p. 303.

page 14
Illustration from Walter C. Burket, ed., *Surgical Papers by William Stewart Halsted:
1852–1922*. Plate L. Halsted was the inventor of the radical mastectomy.
"It's almost a miracle," etc.: Nixon and his loyal secretary, Rose Mary Woods,
White House tape, June 12, 1973.
"Well, to me, clandestine": Sally J. Harmony's testimony, SSC, bk. 2, p. 470.

page 15
"The pain of separation": Lorde, pp. 25–26.
"Reality-testing": Sigmund Freud, "Mourning and Melancholia," *The Standard
Edition of the Complete Psychological Works of Sigmund Freud*, vol. XIV, James
Strachey, trans. and ed. (London: The Hogarth Press, 1962), p. 244.

"[T]he contemporary coagulation": Rachel Blau DuPlessis, "Manifests." *diacritics* 26:3–4 (1996), p. 37.

page 16

"Ponder what may haue passed": *A Manuall of Devout Meditation and Exercises: Instructing How to Pray Mentally. Drawn for the Most Part, Out of the Spirituall Exercises of S. Ignatius. Divided into Three Bookes. Written in Spanish by the R.F. Thomas de Villa Castin of the Society of Iesus. And Translated into English by H.M.* [Henry More] *of the Same Society* (Saint-Omer: English College Press, 1624), pp. 420–21.

"male/female polarization": See DuPlessis, p. 49.

page 18

"Consider vvhome thou cherishest": *A Manuall*, p. 102.

"I don't think there are any living": Testimony of Rose Mary Woods, Friday, May 22, 1974. SSC, bk. 22, p. 10200.

page 19

"1. Repression," etc.: Collette Ray and Michael Baum, *Psychological Aspects of Early Breast Cancer* (New York: Springer-Verlag, 1985), pp. 29–31.

"Is the reader only an observer of tragedy?" For a brilliant response to this question, see Todd Carmody's "The Banality of the Document: Charles Reznikoff's *Holocaust* and Ineloquent Empathy," *Journal of Modern Literature* 32:1, pp. 86–110. "The reader or listener, [Reznikoff] writes, is able 'to feel actually what happened' when concrete particulars take precedence . . . but only as a spectator. . . . To dissolve all barriers between 'spectators' and victims is to be guilty of an altogether different kind of negligence" (102).

"1. Daniel Schorr, CBS, etc.": Composite of several White House enemies lists, from SSC exhibit 49, bk. 4, p. 1695; and SSC exhibit 60, bk. 4, pp. 1716 & 1720.

page 20

"This new body-self": Then how presume to imagine the suffering of the other, that which you (perforce) will never undergo? Exercises like those of Ignatius Loyola, or the Stations of the Cross, are of course designed to aid the practitioner in doing just that. Or maybe just sympathology. Necromanticism. L ck.

"one day you will have to": Based on testimony of breast cancer patients about looking at their own bodies for the first time after their mastectomies. In *You Are Not Alone* [radio program], Edward Janus, producer (Voice Arts, 1998).

"a puckered, ugly slit": Kushner, p. 348.

"We didn't think that probably": Magruder's testimony, SSC, bk. 2, p. 804.

"thick reptilian hide," etc.: Rosamond Campion, *The Invisible Worm: A Woman's Right to Choose an Alternative to Radical Surgery* (New York: Macmillan, 1972), p. 13, describing effects of radiation treatments. I have also echoed the words of "D.M." in a letter to Campion, quoted in Barron H. Lerner, M.D., *The Breast Cancer Wars: Hope, Fear, and the Pursuit of a Cure in Twentieth-Century America* (New York: Oxford Univ. Press, 2001), p. 159. I can barely write this.

"Just about the time": Lorde, p. 38.

"Jeane Dixon tells us": Woods to Nixon, on May 14, 1973, tape.

"Mourning is regularly the reaction": Freud, p. 243.

"Mr. TALMADGE": SSC, bk. 6, p. 2601. But did the boy know who Talmadge *was*—what he'd done as governor of Georgia? Did he know about daddy Talmadge? Or Ervin's railing against open housing and civil rights? They weren't exactly Albert Gore . . .

"If done under your assurance": Ehrlichman's handwritten comment, next to his initial, "E," approving proposal for creation of "Plumbers" unit. SSC exhibit 90, bk. 6, p. 2645.

"Going back to the analogy": Kushner, p. 230.

"Sen. Connally called": To Nixon on tape, June 5, 1973.

"Senator ERVIN": Sen. Sam Ervin, during John Dean's testimony, Wednesday, June 27, 1973, bk. 4, p. 1458. "In this Nation, we have had a very unfortunate fear . . . Now, I think that all grew out of this complement of fear, did it not, the whole Watergate incident?" (Ervin to Macgruder, SSC, bk. 2, p. 855).

"Mommy's sad": From *"Will Mom Be OK?" Families Talk About Breast Cancer* [television program] (Lemont, Ill.: Bosom Buddies, Inc., 2003).

"The concept of total kill": R. M. Kelley, "What Chemotherapy Should be Used in Metastatic Breast Cancer?" *Breast Cancer: A Challenging Problem*, ed. M. L. Griem et al. *Recent Results in Cancer Research 42* (New York: Springer-Verlag, 1973), p. 141.

"I began by telling the President": Testimony of John Dean, Monday, June 23, 1973. SSC, bk. 3, p. 998.

Photocopy of photograph of either G. Gordon Liddy or Howard Hunt "in disguise," prior to the botched burglary of Daniel Ellsberg's psychiatrist's office.

SSC exhibit 146, bk. 9, p. 3866.

"Kids will know": Rev. Amy Snedeker, in *"Will Mom Be OK?"*

page 26

"In order to keep": Kushner, p. 333.

"It was my particular concern": Dean's testimony, SSC, bk. 3, p. 998.

page 27

"The loss of hair": Cancer patient, in *You Are Not Alone.*

"They feel literally deformed": Ray and Baum, p. 20. All these clever boys w/o
    bodies . . .

"Ponder, what is the end of all beauty": *A Manuall*, p. 96.

page 28

"Well, we have an awful lot of things": Sen. Lowell Weicker, Tuesday, July 31,
    1973. SSC, bk. 8, p. 3107. "I have seen so many lives just so completely shat-
    tered" (SSC, bk. 8, p. 3130).

"It just makes me gag": John Dean to John Ehrlichman, transcript of phone con-
    versation re FBI Director L. Patrick Gray's testimony. SSC exhibit 102, bk. 7,
    p. 2951. It's very important to try to get this right.

"Well, I think we ought to let him hang": Ehrlichman to Dean, op cit.

page 31

"the agencyless, choiceless": Du Plessis, p. 40.

"I started to have nightmares": Steven Hess, in *Summer of Judgment: The Water-
    gate Hearings* (television program), WETA Boston, 1983.

page 34

"She kept going": Cf. Virginia Foster Durr, *Outside the Magic Circle* (Tuscaloosa:
    Alabama University Press, 1985): "That's the way Southern women have so
    often met a difficult situation—just acted as though it hadn't happened"
    (p. 267).

"Things are going to change now": Nixon re FBI, White House tape, Sept. 15,
    1972. Part of the so-called "smoking gun tape."

"—and I thought it was time": Dean's testimony, SSC, bk. 3, p. 1000.

page 35

"After Inouye's questioning": Howard K. Smith, *ABC Evening News*, July 25,
    1973.

page 36

"Mr. FRIEDMAN": Milton Friedman, then a White House speechwriter, to
    freelance reporter and breast cancer activist Rose Kushner, re First Lady

Betty Ford's impending radical mastectomy. Quoted in Kushner, p. 372.

"A VOICE FROM THE AUDIENCE": United States Congress, House Judiciary Committee, *Debate on Articles of Impeachment*, 93rd Congress, 2nd sess. H. Res. 803 (Washington: GPO, 1974), p. 140.

"Mr. HESS": Commentator Steven Hess, upon leaving Public Broadcasting Service's coverage of the Watergate hearings, July 23, 1973.

"Mr. DOWNIE": Leonard Downie, *Washington Post* editor, quoted in Michael Schudson, *Watergate in American Memory: How We Remember, Forget, and Reconstruct the Past* (New York: Basic Books, 1992), pp. 108–9.

"Mr. NIXON": Nixon on tape, Feb. 6, 1973.

page 37

Linoleum block print of Magi, Elizabeth P. Harrington, c. 1970.

page 38

"This I am not really definite on": Harmony's testimony, SSC, bk. 2, p. 459.

II. RESIGNATION

New York Times (NYT) citations refer to the dates indicated in the text.

page 43

"SENSITIVE MATERIAL": Liddy's homemade cover for "Gemstone" files. SSC Exhibit 18, bk. 2, 890.

"That dealt with some sort of a drug": Harmony's testimony, SSC, bk. 2, p. 472.

page 45

"some of the concepts": Dean's testimony, SSC, bk. 3, p. 929.

page 46

"Ruby 1 Ruby 2," etc.: Liddy's code words. From Dean's testimony, Wednesday, June 27, 1973. SSC, bk. 4, p. 1512.

"fatigue, restlessness, frustration," etc.: James Reston, describing mood in Washington. NYT, p. 87.

"maybe a scenario": Rep. C. W. Bill Young (R-FL), referring to the outcome of the House Judiciary Committee's impeachment hearings. NYT, p. 1.

"every major substantive part": Sen. Lowell Weicker re Watergate's effects on the Constitution. "[I]f I am emotionally wrought up at this point in time it is because these things have been imputed or an attempt has been made . . ." (this on August 1, 1973). SSC, bk. 8, p. 3174. They didn't know all the details, but they knew something was terribly wrong.

"My mind is not a tape recorder": Dean's testimony, SSC, bk. 4, p. 1373. Elsewhere Dean tells the committee that his memory is excellent. Which it was.

"Senator BAKER": During Dean's testimony, SSC, bk. 4, p. 1482.

"each single one": Freud, 244.

"growing cynicism and apathy": Arthur J. Goldberg re public perception of impeachment hearings. NYT, p. 35.

"TAPE ERASURE": If you're younger than I am, then you will have forgotten all about this.

"Well, I'd cut the loss fast": President Nixon to Haldeman and Ehrlichman, White House tape, June 30, 1972.

"air of saddened defeatism": James M. Naughton, describing Nixon's defenders on Judiciary Committee. NYT, p. 69.

"You don't know what the word": Ervin to John Ehrlichman, former counsel to the President. Tuesday, July 24, 1973. SSC, bk. 6, p. 2579.

"Rose Kushner begins assembling": see Kushner, p. 349.

"We're all emotionally drained": Rep. Tom Railsback, quoted in NYT, p. 12.

"whereupon everything that was touched was corroded": Sen. Lowell Weicker's characterization of White House activities, Tuesday, July 31, 1973, SSC, bk. 8, p. 3131. This statement provoked an outburst of near-murderous rage from the otherwise bland Haldeman.

"moved swiftly": James M. Naughton re Judiciary Committee, NYT, p. 1.

"The new cases of breast cancer every year": A. Hamblin Letton, "The Challenge of Breast Cancer." *Breast Cancer: A Challenging Problem*, ed. M.L. Griem, et al. (New York: Springer-Verlag, 1973), p. 2.

"I did make the assumption": Macgruder's testimony, SSC, bk. 2, p. 793.

"Gather hence a great feare and terrour": *A Manuall*, pp. 88–89.

page 59

"respiration of sky": "The death of a beautiful woman is, unquestionably, the most poetic subject in the world" (Poe). "Angels—twice descending / Reimbursed my store— / Burglar! Banker—Father! / I am poor once more!" (Dickinson). "To die is different than what anyone supposed, and luckier" (Whitman).

"without going into the details": Nixon's instructions to Haldeman, on June 23, 1972, tape, on what to say to the FBI re Watergate. The smoke from the smoking gun.

page 60

"how perplexed and troubled": *A Manuall*, p. 88.

"there was an air of relief": David Rosenbaum, NYT p. 73.

"And now a wave of melancholy tranquility": Sen. John Tower, quoting the end of *Antigone*, in NYT, p. 69.

page 61

"I can understand the English language": Ervin's riposte to an Ehrlichman riposte to an Ervin statement. Tuesday, July 24, 1973. SSC, bk. 6, p. 2576.

page 62

Astrology chart: Many thanks to Lark.

"H. You've got a helluva memory, man": SSC exhibit 149, bk. 9, p. 3881. Heading (in original): "Conversation [of Howard Hunt] with Lucien Conein, July 9, 1971." Everyone has a helluva memory but me.

page 63

"Neyther was there any who woold go": *A Manuall*, p. 403.

"against every instinct": Nixon, in resignation speech, describing his decision to resign.

page 65

"Now what the hell do I do?" SSC exhibit 34-28, bk. 3, p. 1233.

page 67

"The year 1974": Lerner, *Breast Cancer Wars*, p. 170.

"Nobody will ever write a book": Nixon, in maudlin, boozy farewell address to staff, Aug. 9, 1974: "Nobody will ever write a book, probably, about my mother. Well, I guess all of you would say this about your mother: My mother was a saint. . . . Yes, she will have no books written about her. But, she was a saint."

page 68

"AUGUST 8, Mon. 1938": Lib's journal entry for that date.

"Nixon Resigns": This photograph, and that on the following page, by Lauren Porter, Scholar Services, University of Kansas.

page 69

"Well, you can see whether the subject matches the verb": Passage interspersed with snippets of Harmony's testimony. SSC, bk. 2, p. 486.

"Do not be dead": Kay Boyle, "For An American," *Collected Poems of Kay Boyle* (Port Townsend, Wash.: Copper Canyon Press, 1991), p. 20.

page 71

"Never. Never, her name was never mentioned again": "Sheryl," one of Davidman's respondents, referring to lack of family discussion of mother after her death; p. 65.

"Washington . . . willing, and almost eager to forget": James Reston, NYT Aug. 9, 1974, p. 3.

"these individuals are never quite sure": Davidman, p. 102.

"Senator, that is just a thing": Part of Haldeman's outburst against Weicker's previously cited statement. SSC, bk. 8, 3131.

About the Author

JOSEPH HARRINGTON is an associate professor of English at the University of Kansas. He is the author of *Poetry and the Public: The Social Form of Modern U.S. Poetics*, a study of the social meaning of poetry in twentieth-century America (Wesleyan University Press, 2002), and the chapbook *earth day suite* (Beard of Bees, forthcoming). Harrington's poems have recently appeared in *Hotel Amerika*, *Otoliths*, *Fact-Simile*, and *Tarpaulin Sky*, among other periodicals.

Library of Congress Cataloging-in-Publication Data

Harrington, Joseph, 1962-

Things come on : an amneoir / Joseph Harrington.

　p. cm. — (Wesleyan poetry)

ISBN 978-0-8195-7135-9 (cloth : alk. paper)

I. Title.

PS3608.A78175T48 2011

811'.6—dc22　2010043476